LEAD INTO INK

SERIES

LEAD INTO INK
The Breakdown

Poetry by
Alex Joseph

Est. 2017

Alex Joseph Publishing
Burbank, California, U.S.A.
ISBN: 978-0-9988744-0-1
ISBN 10: 0-9988744-0-x
Library of Congress Control Number: 2017942063

Lead Into Ink Book 2 – The Rebuild (Coming Soon)
Follow @leadintoink on Instagram for exclusive updates and
poems not included in the books.

To Alice, my first, last, and only; this one's for you.

Introduction

Lead Into Ink is a three-book series of poems I have written and composed over the years. As far as I can remember, I was always writing on scraps of paper just for the heck of it, never thinking much of it.

Years later, I found myself digging through those same scraps and reliving transient moments that had passed me by. As I transcribed my work, I began to appreciate the collection it had become. From turbulent times to times of adolescent excitement, I had it all recorded. As a promise to myself to leave this life with no regrets and to a leave my future children a legacy they would be proud of, I decided to cross it off my bucket list and to write a book. I try to live life with the idea of permanence and purpose like the ink of a pen, without attribution to accident or fate. Even if it took a while, I know in my heart that I followed my passion.

The first book of the series entitled, *The Breakdown* is a symbol of hard times, sadness, and despair. But more importantly, it is a pathway of purpose, a journey of self-discovery, and believing that there's strength in the breakdown, even if it means starting over. I wear it proudly as a badge of honor of who I am.

I hope you enjoy *Lead Into Ink - The Breakdown.*

Bucket list Before 30

5. Write a Meaningful Book

LEAD INTO INK

Amidst All the Noise

Overwhelmed by my pastimes, I keep myself busy.
Oh, how others consider it a waste of time, *my* time.

Nevertheless, it's fulfilling to me
To tend to these projects and ventures
Because they project light from within
And very much reflect my feelings of self-worth.

I don't know *what* I do it for,
There's no goal. I don't *have to* do this,
But *who* I do it for is unequivocally, for me.
It keeps me sane and quietly occupied.

Once in a while,
It will shut my brain down and
Let me be in the present moment,
Serene and peaceful.

LEAD INTO INK

Not even the blusterous sounds of criticisms
Nor the tumultuous storms of expectations
Disturb me at all.

Because amidst all the noise,
I find time to truly be me.

LEAD INTO INK

Execution

Quite literally,
Do or Die!

LEAD INTO INK

Skyscraper

She was blessed by the City of Angels,
Cast a cloud on her days.
I know she means well,
But her perspective is in shades.

One day I whispered to her
That I'm never ever going to leave,
But then I left on a plane
Headed straight for D.C.

Flashback to the beginning,
She's a product of the 'burbs.
Growing up no silver platters
Laying around, so she heard

Other people speaking so lowly of me.
Rubbing it in my face saying it slowly to me,

LEAD INTO INK

As If I didn't understand that
Failure was expected,
But success was in my mind
So my path was re-directed by her.

I know I told her that
The sky was the limit
Because I believed in my heart.
It took my whole life to build it.

As I gaze at the skyline
From inside of a building,
Wishing I was on the roof
Or at least past this glass ceiling.

Well, the truth of the matter is
She was broken and shattered,
Fell victim to the critics' negativity,
But no matter.

LEAD INTO INK

I threw her up to the heavens
In a whole other atmosphere,
She came crashing down in the heat,
They shouted "Cavalier!"

Buried in the rubble and dust
She cried, "I've had enough."
I picked her off the ground
And said, "We're never giving up!"

I saw it in her face,
She was plagued with a heavy heart,
A soldier reminded of the fight
In his battle scars.

My own blood and sweat
Staring straight into a mirror,
A reflection of myself,
This is my last chance to save her.

LEAD INTO INK

But I will never change her,
Even if the sky decides to scrape her.

LEAD INTO INK

Apollo's Chariot

As the brightly colored sun descends
Upon the eerie sound of trembling waves,
I stand alone in the sunset, not having
Accomplished what I set out to do.
My shadow gains ground becoming one with the
night.

How this cyclical process turns dreamers to stone.
Ambition, back in your cage, tomorrow we roam.

LEAD INTO INK

Tongue Tied

We don't choose who, but we always know when.
I can only describe it as "nervousness" then.

Every part of me shattered into pieces so familiar.
I stood staring upon little mirrors reflecting
impressions of you, like I had seen your soul before
in another space and time.

Overridden by an untamable obsession to engage,
my vulnerabilities rushed to the forefront, more than
I wanted to then.

My heart and my mind met perpendicular to my
mouth only to be halted by my twisted tongue.

That was only the beginning, our story: day one

LEAD INTO INK

Loud Silence

I got a story to tell, that needs to get through.
If only you could hear me, if only you knew.
The incident was quick, quick as a flash.
I looked into your eyes and never looked back.

No words were spoken, but the action was loud.
I could hear my heart pounding, but you didn't hear
a sound.
I kept a poker face on, kept my feelings low key,
Turned to my right and saw you looking at me.

I was scared at first, I admit to myself.
Maybe now I can tell you just how I felt.
My heart's in my mouth, I'm ready to speak,
But when you're around, my voice becomes weak.

LEAD INTO INK

Weak because you're near me.
Scared because you'll hear me.
So the things I want to say,
Begin to drift further away.

I'm scared of the pressure that this puts on you.
If only you could hear me, if only you knew.

LEAD INTO INK

Silence

Silence is golden.
Silence is patient.
Silence is hurtful.
Silence is inquisitive.
Silence is aloof.
Silence is the boldest of reactions, a safeguard from
retraction.

Silence is weakness.
Silence is protection.
Silence is the absence of sound to the recipient, but
not necessarily of its holder.
Silence is a sound of its own that captures an entire
room, but subsides instantaneously with perversion.

LEAD INTO INK

Silence is a weapon; we oft point to ourselves.
Silence, if not meant to mean nothing, stays alive in
our grave, a parasite, feeding on the words that never
made it out.

There is a time to be silent, surely.
But may it never consume you to only
live within the walls of your mind.
For even the rich can starve from gold,
Ask King Midas.

LEAD INTO INK

A Lonely Invitation

When you're feeling lost and lonely,
With nowhere to go,
You turn around looking
For someone you already know.

Hoping that a loved one will come just in time,
To be there beside you and make sure you're alright.

The world has turned dark, a blanket of black.
You wish you could run, but you cannot react.
Your mind now heavy, depressed, and in pain.
You try to remember how you'd lost your own way.

You fear the worst will happen all over again,
But you open your beating heart and
Still you let people in.

LEAD INTO INK

The Night

The night is quite lonely and eerie some say,
And surely in darkness, you'll be taken away.

But it keeps me company, when I'm all alone,
Gives me time for self-reflection, truly some time on
my own.

An ear that always listens even to the back of my
mind, in its cracks and imperfections, absent
criticism of any kind.

The stars give me hope for impossible tasks,
support me wholeheartedly, no questions asked.

The wind passes my window, with a simple hello,
But as its own form of disruption, I ask it to go.

LEAD INTO INK

I never feel lonely here like I do in the day.
No filtering thoughts, my tongue lashes away,
As my soul peacefully transcends this body of mine,
Without restraint of this space and time.

LEAD INTO INK

Special Purpose

When you're around *that person*, you feel special. It makes you realize that maybe you're somebody. I mean *really* somebody, out there in the world. You're so busy with life and you come off as a happy-go lucky person, when deep down, when you have time to unwind, you realize that you're alone. What's worse than being alone? You can't answer that question because your mind is focused on what you have planned for tomorrow or making up for what you couldn't finish today.

There it is back to the stress again to deter you from facing the reality of each night. In fact, you go through a checklist of all you've done, just to justify being alone, because surely you should be counting your blessings. But what you've *done* contributes nothing to *who you are*, only to *what you've done*.

LEAD INTO INK

You're so quick to make judgements about others, but you're afraid to confront yourself. Or is it really just to comfort yourself?

You, just talking to you is sweet. You listen and I love that about you. Maybe the person I want to be has nothing to do with *me*.

LEAD INTO INK

Accidental

I have worked hard in my life, I assure you of that.
But never as hard as I did to share accidental eye
contact.

LEAD INTO INK

Excuse Me Miss

Excuse me miss, my sincerest apologies,
Waiting on a friend to come back? A possibility.
Although a moment of your time is all I really need
To compliment your eyes and the beauty that's
alluded me.

I'm telling you *"You're beautiful,"* honestly though,
the way the dimples in your cheeks curl when I first
said, *"Hello, Miss."*

See, I've been waiting to ask what your name is.
"By the way, I'm Alex and did I mention? I'm not an
expert on clothes, but I noticed the necklace,
bracelet, and earrings that you chose."

I'm attracted to the details, intrigued by your looks,
I want to fall in love with not the cover, but the book.

LEAD INTO INK

Never: Myself and You

Never have a girlfriend, never believe in true love,
Never placed myself second, never regretted every
moment alone,
Never kept my walls down, never needed to fill the
empty,

Never gave my all, never gave my heart away
willingly,
Never needed to trust, never believed in "us,"
Never took a chance, never felt so sure,
Never made a promise, never said I love you
forever.

They say *never say never* because never is never
true.
I say replace "never" with "I", and that's my plan for
you.

LEAD INTO INK

Ownership

Spill your soul on my shoulder and never be alone.
As I do the same, here's a love we can own.

LEAD INTO INK

Every Morning

I see the white picket fence across the front yard,
A place to go home to after working so hard.
I pull into the driveway, awaiting your face
And give you a kiss as I walk through our space.
I take off my shoes as I head for the room.
I sit on the mattress, not wanting to move.
Take off my socks and place them on the ground,
Sit there motionless, not hearing a sound.
I head for the shower and turn on the water.
It's freezing cold, so I wait until it gets hotter.
I finish my business and then I get dressed.
I'm really tired today, I could use some real rest.
I look at your face and wish you goodnight.
Stay up a little longer to make sure you're alright.
Then I doze off to sleep with an extra pillow or two.
Wake up the next morning and thank God, I have you.

LEAD INTO INK

Room for Solace

Any room for solace?

I can only transcend this reality so often, before the temptation of my quest becomes irresistibility too dangerous to pursue.

Had I been uncharacteristic in my actions, I would have faltered quickly to the sirens of my mind. Oh, how guarantees of this world exist only in the mind of the naive. Permission to succeed is the nail in the coffin of what is still alive and breathing.

Still, I ask myself what is driving me? Surprisingly, I struggle to formulate a plausible answer to satisfy my own curiosity.

LEAD INTO INK

And so I continue to contemplate in my mind, as my heart valiantly beats to the sound of its own drum, pursuing an end that it has not yet seen.

In this room for solace, the burgundy couch lies untouched, with dust as its only welcomed guest. Its purpose mundane. For the only person in the room begrudgingly denies its existence, as if to do so, would raise his white flag of defeat.

So on his feet he stands, trying to decipher the future as many have before. Heavily reliant on the collection of his own experiences and voices of those consulted.

Where in this room has he found solace? Nowhere, I'm afraid. At least it's written, the reality of it all. Four walls and the manifestations of his thoughts, in what was intended to be a room for solace.

LEAD INTO INK

Anxiety

It abducts you, reckless and impulsive,
like an onslaught of soldiers raiding your mind
with unheeding disregard for your current state of
being.

Intended for defense, but feeling like submissive
compliance, your body tightens up, as shivers
develop and quake into full blown seizures on the
inside, that no one can see.

From the outside, you're composed and in control.
But as you start to break down from the intense
pressure and stress, in one last valiant attempt to
salvage peace of mind, you find yourself looking for
corners in a circle of chaos, yielding to the inevitable,
submitting involuntarily, ultimately controlled by
Anxiety.

LEAD INTO INK

Solitude

Only in solitude can you find yourself
Because there's no one else to find there.

LEAD INTO INK

Why Write?

Why write what you can say?
Because we retain the feelings and discard the words
away.
We process what we've felt, content we choose to
stay.

But when I write, I prescribe with meaning for
diction to convey.
So when this pen leaves evidence may its articulation
be permanent.
For if it's meant to interpret, then allow the words it's
sacrosanct.

They say, "*A picture is worth a thousand words*", be
it as it may.
So tell me why a painter paints, what's a camera click
away?

LEAD INTO INK

Bite the Bullet

I took a shot, pulled the trigger,
On a dream long ago.
Now I have to bite the bullet
Before it blasts a hole in my throat.

LEAD INTO INK

Icarus

"You have a very bright future."
Oh, how I believed it.
I was consumed by its forecast,
Obsessively focused on the light.

Never did my eyes detract from its eminence
as it intensified profusely in each wake of my being.
Soon squinting and forcing my eyelids open became
one in the same.

Blinders on, tunnel vision, raw exuberant
anticipation of the accomplishment.
What was happening in the periphery was of no
concern to me until...
Suddenly, darkness.

LEAD INTO INK

I found myself reaching for a light, no longer there.
So I projected images pulled from my memory
attempting to revive the radiance I've grown
accustomed to.

But my eyes knew its inauthenticity, the feeling
begotten from an undying passionate fire, knows no
fabrication.

Aware, but only alive in my ignorance, I was surely in
denial.
I hoped to delay confrontation with the painful
reality that my mind accepted and understood as the
truth.

I felt the hot wax of Icarus' wings melt onto my back,
burning disappointment on my skin in all of its
taboo.

LEAD INTO INK

Unable to comprehend the speed of my descent,
My freefall from destiny's pen to a subjugated
annihilation of my last ounces of hope.
A thousand days and nights wasted.

For in mere seconds,
Wax hardened my shortcomings,
And with it, my hope to fly again.

LEAD INTO INK

Kickback

I got no handouts, just kickbacks to show for.
Potential means nothing, when you got nothing you
had worked for.

Work? No problem. Due diligence, the extra mile.
Here I stand miles out. I've been waiting for a while.

Faith, they said believe it.
I did, when I received it.
A blessing from God, they would say, "*Use it as a
gift.*"
My empty hands, now clenched tightly into fists.

Giving up is not easy, but that's not what I did.
Blood, sweat, tears, and burned bridges, that's what I
did.

LEAD INTO INK

Health problems overcame, excuses I'm sure to
some, but with no strength left in the tank, I called
out to courage.
Maybe it'd help with the current, change the sails,
change direction.

So I lay caution to the wind, to do it again four times,
But with no more money to spend, only faith to
depend, I was kicked back again.
Tears of pain bled into the ink of my pen.

What was I to do now? With time wasted, not spent.

And then of course, she was let go.
Perfect timing, exceptional.
Her and I, we're going to make it,
Every day we might as well try because
I'll always have her back, as she does with mine.

LEAD INTO INK

Suitcase

Love isn't a possession, you don't own it.
It's not yours to keep, but you can give it freely,
As it sits among the trinkets in your suitcase.

See only others can give you what you seek to fill,
But it can only come from another.

You cannot grab it or take it,
But you may feel around its edges and take in the
light it emits, absorbing its energy like when the sun
hits your skin.

The only problem is this:
Love is one of many trinkets, not all of them good.

LEAD INTO INK

Pain, loss, and despair are housed in the same
confines,
But, oh does love have so much to share.

Overtime as naivety and the reality of this world
shatters what's pure and love gets lost, overshadowed
by trinkets you have to endure, remember this:

Always put love towards the front as a constant
reminder that what another sees as your baggage is
nothing you and your suitcase cannot overcome.

Carry on.

LEAD INTO INK

Room for Real Estate

I wrote my life in pencil, but wrote your name in
pen.
My pages were half empty and you helped me fill
them in.
And then you picked it up and read it twice, front to
back
And in your comfort, retrieved the pieces I ripped
at.

You gave me reason to relive the darkest pain and
sorrows,
With the promise from your lips, you'd be there for
me tomorrow.
You broke me into chapters, not for rhyme or
reason
Saying, "*Even life goes in cycles, does the year not
have four seasons?*

LEAD INTO INK

You're in this universe to leave your mark, an inscription.
So do not rob yourself of who you are, don't be vain in your existence."

I bled words onto paper, an open discourse to my feelings.
Real estate in my mind, a casket repurposed as a ceiling,
Where I could house my thoughts, and live with myself.
I knew I was never alone and felt comfortable searching for heaven in hell.

And now that room I never used, some feelings I did hide
With thoughts before of hedonism of Dorian's life I'd like.

LEAD INTO INK

And when she found it, she locked herself in the
room all alone.
I knew at once, I felt it then, for such temptations I
atone.

Then one day, after several passed, and in my
anticipation,
She came right out, invited me in, my mind in
preparation.
A burst of light came shining through, a mirrored
self-reflection.
There it was carte blanche, a new home that was
ours, at last I found my direction.

LEAD INTO INK

Q&A

Don't question yourself, it's not worth your time.
Answers will come, let 'em catch up from behind.
Just keep living your life, your path, your destiny.
You deserve to be happy, if not now, then
eventually.

LEAD INTO INK

Today

Preserve the past, but learn to die
With the regrets of yesterday.
Having tomorrow, another day,
To change what you can and
To leave what you can't.
Fate is in His heavenly hands.
With full force of each passing day,
Simply learn to say, "I did what I could today,
Today."

LEAD INTO INK

On an Island Off the Coast

On an island off the coast, I'm retiring from my
work, just in time to see the horizon of a new
beginning.

I have not been myself lately...
Actually, I have, but not the part I like.

Obsession an understatement, disappointment a
constant, and satisfaction thoroughly lacking,
That's the person I am in this moment of self-
acknowledgement.

On an island off the coast, I'm sitting on a mountain
Not of grass, but of sand, that has found its way
between my toes.

LEAD INTO INK

The lullaby of the ocean in harmony with the
piercing crash of the waves before me,
My own personal metronome.

I begin removing the long stocky columns of
confinement surrounding me,
Knowing that very soon there will be a storm.
I remind myself that there is greatness in
preparation, excellence in execution, and self-
contentment in love.

On an island off the coast, I am prepared to leave
everything I know to pursue something more.

LEAD INTO INK

90 Seconds

I once heard that a five-year friendship
Is the byproduct of one and a half minutes
Of unadulterated, intentional speech.

Looking back, have I erected that many walls
With such a short bridge between us?
Or do I hoard minutes like sand...
Just to say, "Yes, I do have a friend."

LEAD INTO INK

Sugar

Oh brother in Christ, my family, my friend.
That's the last I heard of you,
You promised me.
But I expected more from you.

There's so much that I said to you.
Like a scalding hot cup of tea
I doused you, with its contents.
Right before it reached your skin,
I knew I couldn't take it back
and I was okay with that.

Sure it wasn't pleasant, it wasn't meant to be.
It was a direct unadulterated rant of pure and raw
emotion.

LEAD INTO INK

Should I have waited and rationalized my thoughts?
Yes.
But I had grown accustomed to living without a filter,
having seeped my feelings, just moments before.

Being with you, I mean just being around you,
was something short of indescribable, a familiar vibe
that I could never get used to, *jamais vu*.
It was the first time, every single time.

It was knowing what was going to happen and how I
was going to feel, but even with its acquaintance, I
was never fully prepared for it.

So when you left, I retracted and recommissioned
higher walls.

I paved a direct path for you to leave,
Carved with the sharpness of my tongue.

LEAD INTO INK

I wanted you to hear it.
You felt it, you left.

We used to sit across from one another each
with a cup of tea.
I always added sugar, lightly stirred.
I knew it was not enough to fully dissolve,
but my attention was on you.
You knew better than I did, I was there for the
company.

Now I sit alone in this shop with an empty cup,
Yet there remain remnants of sugar that never got
stirred.

I never got to tell you all the sweet parts.
I never got to tell you how enamored I was.
I never liked tea anyways,
I stayed for the sugar.

LEAD INTO INK

Good vs. Evil

Feeling the ceiling, but not seeing the roof,
A dance with the devil in his cunning pursuit.
Ill will took a sip of the King's bloody cup.
The world took it in and then threw it back up.

It crashed before it fell into the hands of thine Eve,
As a piece of your mind was infected by greed.
Subtle and young, but too strong to withstand,
Held in His palm, in the palm of His hand.

A serpent, an apple, built upon this rock, this chapel
A choice, well in fact, to decide *who am I in this
battle?*

48

LEAD INTO INK

Writing

Ink drenched on the paper, red marks on the side.
Some words are crossed off, every word so precise.
The meaning is clear, I see it in my head,
But I write too fast, I get too far ahead.

Communication is key for the writer's success.
How am I to properly deliver this message
With all these words jumbled up in a mess?

Each word plays a role, in forming the piece,
Making sure each line is defined and complete.
The image is portrayed through the words I've
selected,
Making sure that the reader and writer are always
connected.

LEAD INTO INK

Because the message should be clear or open-ended at least.
Let the reader taste each bite of this word-written feast.

LEAD INTO INK

The Harbor

I harbor dreams along the sea and you my company.
The light that shines between the fog dances in the
breeze.
And as I peer upon the port along the periphery,
The smell of pungent rotting dreams greets me
eerily.

For what lies ahead I cannot see, remains a mystery.
But if I flee and if I leave, will it put my soul at ease?
The waves will crash, my soul will last, today I will
not freeze.
So on this boat I'll stay afloat and with me are my
dreams.

LEAD INTO INK

Index

90 Seconds — 44
Accidental — 19
Amidst All the Noise — 1-2
Anxiety — 26
Apollo's Chariot — 8
Bite the Bullet — 29
Every Morning — 23
Excuse Me Miss — 20
Execution — 3
Good v. Evil — 48
The Harbor — 51
Icarus — 30-32
Kickback — 33-34
A Lonely Invitation — 14
Loud Silence — 10-11
Never: Myself and You — 21
The Night — 15-16

On an Island Off the Coast — 42-43
Ownership — 22
Q&A — 40
Room for Real Estate — 37-39
Room for Solace — 24-25
Silence — 12-13
Skyscraper — 4-7
Solitude — 27
Special Purpose — 17-18
Sugar — 45-47
Suitcase — 35-36
Today — 41
Tongue Tied — 9
Why Write? — 28
Writing — 49-50

LEAD INTO INK

Lead Into Ink Book 2- The Rebuild: Coming Soon!

For the latest updates and exclusive offers,

Follow
Instagram: @leadintoink
Facebook: facebook.com/leadintoink
Twitter: @leadintoink